The Secret Life
of
Hardware

Poems by
Cheryl Lachowski

FutureCycle Press
futurecycle.org

Acknowledgments

The title for this collection was blatantly lifted from Vicki Cobb's book of science experiments for kids.

The last line in "Switch" is based on a quote from Emily Dickinson: *If I feel physically as if the top of my head were taken off, I know <u>that</u> is poetry.* "Switch" is dedicated to Dwight Ashley whose music does just that.

Cover art by mdilsiz

Cover and chapbook design by Diane Kistner,
dkistner@futurecycle.org

Published by FutureCycle Press
Mineral Bluff, Georgia, USA

ISBN 978-1-938853-20-3

Table of Contents

Fuse

Everything in me mutters *burn:*
each day
the misplaced,
forgotten, uncooperative, broken.

The wick
runs through the face
of the Buddha   who said:
make yourself into a resistant
wire
          take
all great and small
disasters
into your heart, become
an open circuit:
continuous, complete.

I light
the match.

Switch

Thich Nhat Hanh,
a Buddhist monk, wrote,
When we are angry,
we are the anger.
If so, when you try to flip
the switch's toggle down,
you merely make the room
go dark. You think, OK,
I'm out of here,
at least that's over.
But it's not. You have to
go back in
without a flashlight, lamp,
or even a candle.
This room's been wired
for sound. You have to listen
to the music of your own
sweet netherworld
until you squirm and fret
and finally the top
of your unenlightened
head flies off.

Chisel

You fault the implement
for what the hand reveals.
But wasn't it you
who fancied your genuine self
hidden within the cedar's heart?
Now heartwood and sapwood
succumb to the wedge
by offering up another mask.
You can't deliberately shape
a totem out of longing.
That bird who is seldom seen
shapes you.

Hacksaw

There is a cave
where the remains
of a cook-fire
smolder in the dark
and a hidden hand
grips a jawbone
with teeth attached
ready to cut through
the iron bars
around your heart.

Rake

in a Japanese

garden: the tranquil

tines shape

patterns of lines

in the sand

aesthetics

is grounded in

perspective:

      in one respect

blind rage depends

on sight

and has its own

stark grace—

that seductive

body or face

which turns

all hearts

      these teeth

drawing blood

Drill

Eros: lover

of logical

holes

once thought to dwell

within the vena

cava, pelvic arch

or solar plexus

now proven by repeated

rotational abrasions

to the skull

to be a vaporous encephalic

manifestation

along the lines of demons,

sprites, and other

combustible humors

which can also at times

surreptitiously

inhabit the breath

of certain poets and

yoga adepts

whose burning

language and kiss can

permanently

brand your lips

Hammer

A thigh bone:

(ideally mammal,

preferably

large, untamable) one

where the inner edge

leads straight

to the body's

root, stem, the whole

blooming tree

and the sky

drums down

down

down until even the birds

fly off in a perfect

delirium

Rope

Laying the rope begins

with those fragrant entanglements

of schisandra, wisteria,

honeysuckle, rose. And strands

of music which loop

around your heart. Then the bonds

words make, and a provocative

touch. But you risk

that same old story: love

and loss of love. Those knots

and their wearing through.

Hinge

Long-joined, what love
there was
worn thin by the relentless
lamentations of wind and rust

Pliers

All too often one of those
unforgotten loves revolves
through disillusionment
like an amusement park ride:
invariably twenty
years younger, no debt,
or illness, or children from a first
or second marriage—
instead the stars that night
are fixed in their imagined
plotlines and the fallen snow
continually covers the path
where the two of us walked,
slid, laughed arm-in-arm
for hours as if we'd never
let go

Level

Not for me:

the world

a bubble

centered

in lemon yellow

light.

Move

a bit

closer. I'm

most alive

when my heart's

askew.

Wrench

Stubborn as a bolt,
nut, pipe that will not
turn, you resist
all blunt or subtle
come-ons. I'm no engineering genius,
but elementary mechanics
claims we gain in power
through rotational
motion. So I'm stepping back—
not for building up
momentum like a runner
at the long jump,
but for that wider arc
because it's very likely
you're the flip side of myopic.
From now on, a greater distance
will describe us: you can be
the axle while I just circle
around and around the outer rim
and risk the centrifugal
force that lets things fly.

Locks

and keys, plugs and sockets

with their worn out

sexual innuendos as if human

connections were merely a matter

of anatomy, although forcible entry

is in all likelihood the actual

oldest profession and the reason

chastity belts play a supporting role

in Truffaut's *The Man Who Loved Women.*

These days a charm would be

more effective against a breach

of etiquette or integrity than any

mechanical system of bolts and bolt-

undoers: a magical spell

with just the proper combination

of words and voice inflection

for an easy *open sesame,*

but even *charm* has been sullied

by references to the beguiling

powers of women and is also currently

applied to quarks as being *charmed,*

defined by Webster's as having 1)

an electrical charge two-thirds times

the electron's charge, 2) a charm quantum

number of one, and 3) more mass

than up, down, and strange quarks,

which returns us to the original

thesis regarding the dissolution

of metaphor in English.

Shovel

Down too deep it's useless—
the blade can scoop and lift
and throw   but your words come back
rebounding off the walls:
you fool   no hope   not now
or ever   good for nothing   failure

the woman of the dunes
imprisoned in her sandpit
had to rig a basket to a pulley
even though she knew the wind and sea
would never cease to shift the ominous
edge of sand above   she only loved
the sky but it was something

Paint

spreads thin. But jazz
can sink right down

below the surface of a funk
like an IV's syncopated drip,

although for some emotions, paint
might also turn the trick:

I've seen a Spier picture book
where three resourceful kids

(their parents *in absentia*)
cheer the house's dull façade,

ransacking the garage
for every can of flat or glossy

hue. And, in the end, boy,
were they ever happy

with their suburban colonial mix
of Jackson Pollock and Seurat.

Even so, I'll go
with a Coltrane sax

or Miles Davis riff
because like me

they're kind of
blue.

File

Ruthless:
calling that overweight
nurse's aide a quivering
blancmange, and your grandson
a bumbling twit, your wife a cur,
your doctor malpractice
waiting to happen

even if it's fear
that's talking, some words
can wear away compassion's
metal threads

Glue

Introduction to Molecular Chem—
Unit Seven: The Intimacy
of Polymers, in which
diversions into historical
discussions of stewing old horses'
skins and hooves will be
discouraged, and the similarity
to the public romantic contortions
of adolescents, whose limbs
extend beneath above around
the armpits to the front and rear
pant's pockets, will be noted.
More lurid and risqué
comparisons will be limited
to fermenting sourdough starter
and Norwegian lutefisk.

Screwdriver

To extract the milk from coconuts,

a handheld kitchen ice pick works

quite nicely for an easy puncture

but produces just a drip, which takes

all day to empty. For an exit

big enough to let the liquid move

more quickly, use your largest diameter

driver, gently tapping with a hammer

so the tapered tip or Phillips scores

the fibrous husk at one eye or another. You can

also smash the whole shebang on concrete

but the milk is history and there's no

assurance you'll end up with perfect halves

to use as bra cups during Jimmy Buffett's

gig for all his parrotheads.

Pipe

It's comforting to know

the neutron bomb has been designed

to spew a host of gamma rays

and neutrons with a weaker blast

than most nuclear explosives—

that way incineration

of anything other than animate

is less likely, and if the walls

and frames of buildings

were to fall, the bones of our elaborate

plumbing systems would stand alone

as testimonials to artistic

avant-garde and human genius.

Crowbar

Surely the resemblance to a crow's foot

is open to question:

for one thing, toes and claws

extend out front in a trinity

of thin and scaly revelations.

And, two, there seems to be

no leverage required

to grip what's left of last night's

roadkill while the keen redemptive

beak performs its crude

but necessary business.

Twopenny Nails

Being the least

and most numerous

among us

it is said

they are blessed

and

like every blade

of grass

have souls

Screws

mathematically conjured

elements of the mysteries

beginning with

Archimedes who could levitate

water by a

helical thread—these days

initiates ascend

a spiral stair

narrow, torchlit, walled

by hand-hewn

stone, their God

continually slipping

out of sight around

the curve that

never ends